I0163066

Absent Nightmare Zinnias: Rhymed Acrostics from A to Z

Linda Ann Nickerson

Absent Nightmare Zinnias:
Rhymed Acrostics
from A to Z

Gait

House

Press

Copyright © 2013 Linda Ann Nickerson

All rights reserved. No part of this book may be reproduced or transmitted in any form or by any means, electronic or mechanical, including photocopying and recording, or by any information storage and retrieval system, without permission in writing from the publisher.

Published in the United States by Gait House Press.

Printed in the United States of America.

2013

ISBN: 0615825990
ISBN-13: 978-0615825991

Cover Illustration: Vintage Botanical, copyright expired/public domain

DEDICATION

This book is fondly dedicated to all of
the wonderful wordsmiths, bibliophiles,
fellow writers, and word lovers who have
touched my life and inspired my craft
throughout my lifetime.

AUTHOR'S PREFACE

What is an acrostic poem?

Acrostic poetry is becoming increasingly popular, perhaps for the simplicity it offers.

Creative writing students often enjoy crafting acrostic verse, as this poetic form offers an easy place to start.

The acrostic poet chooses a key word, and writes it as a vertical column. Those letters become the initials for opening the lines of the poem.

Rhymed acrostics are trickier.

This rarer form of acrostic poetry follows the methodology outlined above, but with the addition of both meter and rhyme.

Rhymed acrostics may be easy to read, but they are considerably more challenging to construct.

I hope readers will enjoy perusing and pondering the acrostic poems that follow. Verse topics range from normal life to nightmares, from careers to curiosities, and from serious subjects to satire.

Linda Ann Nickerson

CONTENTS

1
ABSENT

Anyone may step away

Breaking bonds that once held sway,

Slipping from the inner ring,

Exiting with broken wing.

Nodding heads and shaking fists:

Tell me, will I yet be missed?

2
BAKERY

Blessed bounty boasts to greet -

Aromatic oven treat.

Kneaded, rolled and rising right,

Epicurean delight.

Regularly, I forgo,

Yet today, I can't say, "No."

3
CAREERS

Calendars and callings count.

Aptitudes raise all amount.

Rank recession pulls us back -

Each employee's heart attack.

Economics, heckles raise;

Risk analysis betrays.

"Stop the bleeding!" Nation pays.

4
DAFFODIL

Dear delightful sign of spring,

Always, as your petals fling,

Find we favor, hope's new flash.

Flowers call us from the ash

Of a season, dark and cold.

Daffodil, may you behold –

In our empty tempers, trill.

Look! The promise blooms at will.

5
EAVESDROPPER

Echoes of a private word

At the corner, overheard.

Violated by an ear,

Every confidence to hear.

Secrets may not still be so.

Drunkenly do rumors grow.

Rumbled scandals bear no truth,

Over-shared by slinking sleuth.

Pick your battles. Find your foes.

Play your games as no one knows.

Empathetic list'ners balk.

Richer ones reject your talk.

6
FLANNELS

Favorite finds for cozy dress,

As we dream and decompress.

Vital wardrobe, though it's clear

Out-of-doors, we shan't appear.

Really, folks, this much is true:

I'd wear more, if I were you.

Turn around, and find some clothes.

Even PJs need repose.

7
GUMPTION

Go for triumph. Seek the end.

Understand and apprehend.

Make a promise. Eye the line.

Pick a spot, and stake it thine.

Take a stand, and make a vow.

I'm all-in. Don't stop me now.

Overcomers, stubborn sorts,

Never question good reports.

8
HURRICANE

Have you ever stood in a hurricane,

Under the blast and waves of rain?

Race for the shelter. There abide.

Reach for the loved ones tossed aside.

In a storm, with whirling gust,

Can we congregate? We must.

After all, the tempest blows,

Never warning where he goes,

Ever thrashing friends and foes.

9
INSOMNIA

It irritates me to no end —

No sleep arrives. No dreams descend.

Stop snoring, sonorific one

Or soporific nights are done.

My temper tromps on its last nerve,

Now nudging, as he does deserve.

I cannot rouse the ratchet jaw.

And so I toss and hem and haw.

10
JERKS

Just those who are rather ill-bred

Eclipse every word that is said –

Repeating their own,

Kind manners unknown.

Some say they are merely misled.

11
KINETIC

Kids around here are kinetic.

I might have to summon a medic.

No downshift, no rest.

Each moment a test

To see when we folks grow frenetic.

In time, they their tanks may deplete;

Count ten, and they're back on their feet.

12
LAUGHTER

Lovely laughter lifts me up,

Aids my aura, fills my cup.

Universally, it's true.

Great guffaws are good for you.

Hearty chuckles help us cope.

Twinkles in our eyes bring hope.

Every chortle, crow and whoop

Rallies spirits to regroup.

13
MILEAGE

Many miles have made their mark

In my features: line and arc.

Life has left its learning clear —

Every wrinkle, spot, and smear.

Any day, I'd skip a trade;

Give me every hair that's greyed,

Each dear mem'ry there displayed.

14
NIGHTMARE

Nevermore may I nod off.

In my dreams, the beast may scoff.

Give me rest; need forty winks.

Help! My form is filled with kinks.

Tell soft stories; banish boos.

Make my mind see merry news.

All my energies are naught.

Rest retreats as afterthought.

Eerie sights mean slumber's shot.

15
OVERREACT

Oops! Volcano spews its smoke.

Violence is no jester's joke.

Enemies deserve his rage;

Relatives cannot assuage.

Rationality has run.

Everything has come undone.

All at once, his visage shifts.

Colors dull, and conflict drifts.

Tell me: is it worth the rifts?

16
PACKRAT

Poking through a pile of crates,

Ancient treasures, gifted greats.

Contemplating what to toss,

Keeping diamonds, losing dross.

Recognizing heirloom's bluff –

After all, enough's enough.

Tomorrow I can stow this stuff.

17
QUARRELS

Quacking quitters in a snit –

Unrelenting, throw a fit.

Argue always, if you must,

Realizing, lost is trust.

Rich rewards lie not in right.

Endless evils may excite,

Luring prideful passions out.

Still, the contrite keep their clout.

18
RANDOM

Random thoughts may take a toll,

All attentions to control.

Never underestimate the fee –

Dear distractions, nth degree.

Oh, my goodness, lookie here!

My resolve did disappear.

19
SHRILL

She sits and screams.

Her voice, it seems,

Resounds anew –

Irate, askew.

Let's take a walk.

Look, still she'll squawk.

20
TABLET

This tablet takes me everywhere,

All filled with games and books to spare.

But, mercy me, I've ditched my sight,

Lost lingering in light each night.

Eyes blurred, I rise to face each sun

Too tired to think, by reads undone.

21
UMBRELLA

Underneath my tiny tent,

Mini shelter, time is spent.

Bumbershoot and brolly too,

Rainy days meet spring's debut —

Even in the brightest rays,

Lollygagging, no malaise.

Loving weather, dry or wet,

All my days I pirouette.

22
VANITY

Vacuous though it may be,

All the world is vanity.

Notice not that we be blind,

Ill at ease, and disinclined.

Tell us what we yearn to hear,

Yes, you're simply lovely, Dear.

23
WHATEVER

When having it all takes all that you
have,

How much do you lose, claiming prizes
you crave?

Accomplish all aims to build bounty and
barns.

Turn straw into gold, spinning platters
and yarns.

Escape interactions to chase the
crusade.

Voice every victory; you've got it made,

Except what you've forfeited – stuff you can't count.

Rich treasures? Whatever. Who knows the amount?

24
EXITING

Explorers may not be afraid,

eXcept as they beyond are bade

Into the place where no trail leads.

That destination all exceeds.

I once was blind and chanced to spy

No sight beheld by mortal eye.

Good things await the last goodbye.

25
YIKES

Yon lies one-time stalker, who sought to make fright.

It seems that his bark was much worse than his byte.

King Crybaby Creeper, he posted his mind,

Each message more threatening, yet always unsigned.

Some say his persona concealed his own blight.

26
ZINNIAS

Zippy big blooms, they light up the yard.

Inside, they greet me, my own color guard.

Never need polishing, shiny and bright,

Nature's own fireworks, floral delight.

I till the soil and drop seeds there to rest,

Anticipating the garden's best dressed.

Simply delightful, my zinnias attest.

ABOUT THE AUTHOR

An award-winning poet and prolific writer, holding a B.A. in English and an M.S. in Journalism, Linda Ann has worked as a professional writer for more than three decades. She has also taught creative writing classes.

Linda Ann Nickerson writes news and feature columns for several well-known websites. Her published portfolio includes well over 5,000 web articles, as well as countless print pieces.

Blogs owned by Linda Ann Nickerson include:

Delightfully Amiss: Berzerkians Gone Amok and Finding the Funk in Dysfunction

Heart of a Ready Writer

Nickers and Ink

Practically at Home

The Mane Point

Working in Words

and more.

Readers are invited to follow Linda Ann Nickerson on Twitter (LindaAnnNickers) or Google+ (Linda Ann Nickerson) or to join the Nickers and Ink Facebook page.

www.ingramcontent.com/pod-product-compliance
Lightning Source LLC
Chambersburg PA
CBHW060101050426
42448CB00011B/2571

* 9 7 8 0 6 1 5 8 2 5 9 9 1 *